FAT DAISIES

Fat Daisies
© 2015 Carrie Murphy

Published by Big Lucks Books
Washington, DC
BigLucks.com

ISBN: 978-1-941985-01-4

Cover design by Phillip Nessen
Interior design by Mark Cugini

Titles set in Gill Sans
Text set in Crimson

First edition, September 2015

FAT
DAISIES

CARRIE MURPHY

BIG LUCKS BOOKS 2015

CONTENTS

SILVER PIGLET   I

THE END OF ANTENNAS   2

FILTER   3

GORGONZOLA   4

MONTGOMERY'S GLANDS   5

SUNNIES   6

BLUE RIDGE   7

CANDIED   8

UNIVERSAL   9

POISON ARROWS   II

JUST LOCK ME UP WITH MY NETFLIX QUEUE & LET ME DIE   12

EVEN FROM ACROSS THE OCEAN   13

CREOSOTE   14

HEIGHTS   15

TRIGGER WARNING   16

I AM THE KING OF MY OWN LIFE   17

MOTEL BOULEVARD   22

FAT DAISIES   23

WILD EGG   24

ALL MY TURQUOISE   25

TANG   27

MILLENNIALIST   28

DON'T READ THE COMMENTS   29

FROM ABOVE   30

POEM OF OUR MOMENT   33

DUMB BITCH   35

JAM   36

THINSPO   37

TWENTY ASSES   38

PHOBE MANIFESTO   39

SOMEONE ELSE'S BODY   41

WHY WHITE PEOPLE LOVE
"REMIX TO IGNITION"   43

UNICORN   44

MOON CHART   45

NINE STRAND   48

ALEXANDRIA TO WARRENTON   49

MOUNT VERNON AVENUE 50

BLUELAND 51

LEDGE & HAMMER 52

ROYGBIV 53

SUNKIST 57

LITTLE HAIRS 58

IDEA OF A ROAD 59

SCARF 60

RECEIPTS 61

AKELA FLATS 62

"*But the ladies*
they have so many choices now
they wear high heels they wear sneakers"
—Laura Jaramillo

"*to learn to manage the impact of one's insecurities.*"
— DeRay McKesson

SILVER PIGLET

Each morning I jolt
into my own gigantic smallness.

The underwear I buy to replace
period-stained ones,

eggs & spinach lame
& jaunty on a bright plate.

Hair in the drain. Careful hooks
on the walls, swooping scarves

in the closet. Click through a lens
& sweep through a filter.

Sunspots & stripes. Rows
of herbals, heavy ringlets.

All this having of flesh to be
in, all this yawning inside

my spotted little Eden
where I memorize & trash.

THE END OF ANTENNAS

All afternoon I congratulate myself
on my industrious progress, words swimming
across the screen & plants freshly watered,

the balm for the soul of the meal-planned,
the vacuumed.   That black hole, though.
The asteroids that are out there. All

of the bright bad things that can happen—
my uterus losing its right to itself &
the scorching of California.

Why should I want a bring a baby into this world
where we're running out of water
& we're running out of time?

But medieval people thought the world was going to end, too,
I remind myself. Michelangelo & penicillin
& camera phones were still yet to come
to make us smart & healthy,
to fill our eyes.
Now we are our own auteurs.

The future's slowly turning into yawns across
miles, every day like the beauty of the burnt-
out log in the bosque, the breath of the stoner
boys down the street, their fuzzy dirty hair,
the thick pulsing of their arteries.

My neighbor's tire treads make the unlikely
shape of a heart in the baking brown dirt
so I think it's a sign of the small things,
& how they can keep us safe.
It's the end of the day, the end of the
story, the end of antennas.

FILTER

Sometimes I just want to lie down
& pancake out & become smoothed
so the wheels of shopping carts
can roll on me like on the floor
of Target on a Tuesday.

Everything is a camera
or at least everything is something
to pose for.

I narrate myself to myself
in my head like I did as a child
who always knew she'd be a writer,
although she'd much rather have been an actress
with applause bursting across her face.

Everything is a stage
or at least everything is on a stage
because we carry lights with us in our pockets.

If it's vain to pose
with a click in the mirror,
then I'm vain.
Look at my lipstick,
look at my grin. Here I am. Here I am!

Flatten me. Hold me up.
I'm dressed in the floral romper
sold in three thousand other stores,
& my hands are folded. Now open.
Now closed. Now open.

GORGONZOLA

Here, amongst all the douchebags carrying salads,
I ponder my privilege.

I have so much & yet I want
so much. So, so much.

All my greed is making me
greedier. All my grateful feelings

are giving me other, bigger, grateful
feelings. My big gigantic feelings

& my huge gigantic wanting, a wanting
that puts me to sleep with its dull-edged

normal, its relentless prison-striped
marching on top of each sunshine-y day

at the designer salad bar with nuts! Seeds!
Spinach! Grains from Peru! Fruit from China!

Goodness stacked around me, more
& never enough. Formica, nylon,

patent-leather booties. Airplane mode of the
soul against the 529 plan I didn't ask for

but burnt through with studded drugs & golden books,
finding fake beauty in a wire rack of Dorito bags

pushed to the dirty floor. Room after room
of us, the un-ugly.

MONTGOMERY'S GLANDS

A white baby suckling
at a black breast &
the woman in the lactation
course saying *I don't see
color* as I bite the inside
of my cheek to bare blood
my pink pink cheek
& my prepregnancy pride
that I have *good nipples*
but there's no guarantee
on good. I was taught
that there's no real
wrong answer but there
is. We don't get to sit
around & give opinions
like seeds blowing out
of a dead dandelion.
Not anymore.
I used to police
my face so carefully:
*don't show your
fear* or your joy,
either. But now
I show them,
some.

SUNNIES

I want people to look at me,
but also I don't.
In my striped shorts, I'm writing
at the coffee shop & some girl keeps
glancing, some old man with
eggy sandwich strings caught in his moustache
keeps smiling, & I'm just screaming
fuck you inside my fingers because there's
nothing here to see.

I want to eat pizza when I want to eat pizza.
When I see pizza somewhere, I want to eat it.
When I want to have sex, I want to have sex.
When I'm walking around I want people to
look at me, but only most of the time
& only when I say so. Aren't I the agent
of my agency, after all? Aren't I one with the clam
that jams out, & the pearl, too? *I'm the fucking*
pearl I'm the fucking pearl I said
                    over & over again in my head.

BLUE RIDGE

I don't want to sing
before a crowd
of thick admirers;

I want to scream
into a vase of flowers
out in the country

where all my brittle feelings
go unnoticed, mercied
like the dew on the grass.

My belly, with its blonde hairs
& o, god, the shape of the shaved-head
woman next door

the sloping broken record
of her sadness.
I'm building a tower here.

One for all the buzzes in the air
to call home, their own. One
where the dot-dot-dot can't come.

CANDIED

Is anyone really interested in you
other than your mom?

You'll never get out from under
the gas-scented ghost of Sylvia so stop

trying. Remember that your vagina
& your identification with your vagina

is your currency.
Curse.

Go ahead & didact like you tap
dance. You don't have enough

heart to grieve for everyone
so pick your cause

& start fundraising. You're too old
for crazy-cool self-destruction but

you'll still be seen sniffing bourbon
suggestively for the whiff

of the wild. That bit of violet
that whips

& what you can say about it.
How you can spin.

UNIVERSAL

When you say everyone, meaning everyone, do you really mean
white people? Do you picture white people in your head?

I think I used to but not anymore
but I don't think now makes me any better

than I was before, than what I learned before,
the ESOL kids in middle school singing

"We Are The World" at the talent show while mainstream kids
laughed, how I wanted to cry and punch everyone in the

dark auditorium or when I say everyone likes to shop
by which I mean the click click florescent shine

on the floor of the mall like everyone has the same stores
in their mall, like everyone has the same impulse to push their head

above water in the deep end of the shot-through sunny pool
or put their hand on their phone when there's footsteps behind

like everyone is just the people
I can reach, the ones I think might like me,

or the ones who are like me. The audacity to make
ourselves the rule while getting to say

we're the exception, too, smiling at the happy Latina
mom vacuuming on TV but then buying Dyson anyway,

all the powdered sugar on all the neatly decorated
donuts which are now everyone's donuts,

I mean they're America's donuts because oh right
"the human condition" & we all fuck &

sleep & shit & love & hate, right? Everyone
has a body, a face, a favorite ice cream flavor,

so let us not let our differences divide us
because we're everyone, everyone who was

then us, everyone who is now just that one second:
before you hear the footsteps, before you turn your head.

POISON ARROWS

Every piece of fruit is different than every other piece of fruit
that has ever been in the world. Doesn't that make your head hurt?

I eat ibuprofen every morning so the inside of my head
doesn't feel like staring at hotel wallpaper.

Grey & then pink & then gray & then pink.
A man spitting out a huge quantity of mouthwash next to his car

as I stand there, looking confused. I pull loose strands caught in my hair,
make thick little balls & drop them as I walk.

If they ever want to find me, they can find me.
All my soft bullets of DNA.

JUST LOCK ME UP WITH MY NETFLIX QUEUE & LET ME DIE

Said all the white people when we realized
we could never go home again. We wanted
all our stuff & we wanted our moms smoothing
back the hair from our foreheads
& microwaving tea. We wanted ergonomic
desk chairs. We wanted Gwyneth Paltrow
& we wanted Colin Firth & we wanted British accents
to break over us as we slept, bearing
us away on the tide of colonialism
without guilt.

We wanted Romantic Dramas About Fairy Tale Frogs
& Lusty Comedies Starring Robin Williams
& Movies With A Blue Mood.
But we couldn't have any of it.

We couldn't have popcorn on the couch with a cat purring beside us.
We couldn't have Toblerone bars or leather seats inside our cars.
We couldn't have the best thing ever smothered in hot melty queso.

Because there was nothing left.
No money for our moist organs or glossy hair,
no pretty pens that signed checks like chocolate.

All the blue ribbons of the world
had been rounded up & kept in a big glass jar.

That's what we're supposed to watch now,
to pass the time:
satin on satin on
satin on satin on gold
rubbing,
thin.

EVEN FROM ACROSS THE OCEAN

I saw a picture of this girl I went to college with & thought to myself
That's the prettiest you're ever going to look, K___,

which is mean as snarking on the fleshy little faces
of the children on the mommyblogs I read;

their impossibly droll dresses & knock-kneed
charming inanity like my other

Facebook friend's photos of the oatmeal chin baby she calls
her own baby, how I cried & cried when she adopted

it from Africa, a woman I barely know, a baby from across
an ocean, a cookie I was eating with my happy tears

splashed right on it like I could feel her own sloppy & graceful
& towering joy & call it my own because it was right in front

of my eyes even though it was in a hot, dusty, sunny
place where people were squinting & holding babies

they would make become their own babies with a house full
of plastic & cotton onesies even though maybe they were already

their own babies even from across the ocean & maybe K___ will look
prettier than in the picture with the lace dress where she looks so glowy

like she's her own vase of herself & if she does become more beautiful
I will know it, I will see it when she posts it because of course she will post

it, all of us clicking away, babyless & lit from within.

CREOSOTE

I drive east towards the mountains,
digging dirt from under my fingernails
with my teeth. *I am racist,*
I say to myself. *I am racist,* I say.
I am jealous, I say. *I am jealous*
of the women with babies
& of the women with no fear
& of the poets who are smarter
than I can ever be. I am not
jealous of scientists or spacemen
or men. I am racist in thought
& in deed as hard as
I think I am trying
against word. I am racist reaching
back through centuries
of prizing precious quartz, the lily-lit
china of my white woman's
body. I watch the pink
sun dip lower & leak.
I am using nature as an epiphanic
end. I am not a delicate flower,
cropped. I am not the smell
of the desert after a rain. Neither
are you. I am implicated.
I am a response—
responsible.

HEIGHTS

root root root like a baby for a breast

as I see myself squirm for approval

& how did I end up with a job where I help women
decide how they're going to get their babies
out of their bodies

Isn't that really bougie said the drunk man to me
& I said *I guess so* with a weak apologetic smile
like I need to defend what I do with my time
to some motherfucker

but of course I do feel like I need to define
what I do to motherfuckers
like how I earn my money is anyone's business
but my own but it is because being me or you or she

means having to justify anything like your crocodile
pocketbook or your red-cheeked children & how you got them,
& why. I can write thinkpieces & reload,

hoping for a chorus, but honesty is only one way out.
We're here in the ether, effervescent in our constant reimagining

of what it means to be a person with a checkbook, a conscience,
& a sex drive. *It's harder than I thought* said my friend,
like lonely bursting frustration is a new invention for our age,
head-shaking, a shame, the crazy price of stamps these days

& shoes scattered everywhere on the closet floor
when suddenly someone's toddler bolts forth
& springs out across the yard like water from a hose with a hole,

the sharp embarrassed scream in the scramble to
gather everything, put it back, & zip.

TRIGGER WARNING

Something I eat or something I don't eat;
every day I negotiate

my space. My bright beigeness. My pukeworthy
puce. I like words & phrases in groups of three

so I keep them there with commas & I keep my
stomach flat or full. I am the slip in between

woman & in between. If you call me wrong,
I'll slice. My pubic hair bigger than it ever was

& better, too. I think I don't need anyone to agree
with me but that's also a lie.

I think I'm a tiny woodland creature with gigantic eyes.
I eat shards of glass & light. Shards

of glass & light are always coming up in poems,
right? Representing what's beautiful,

what's broken. I think I want
to represent cheeseburgers,

a fat circle of fat, juicy & contained.

I AM THE KING OF MY OWN LIFE

The dried-up Ss of worm bodies on the sidewalk freak me out

My dog licks them

My dog is the best thing in my life

Better than food or sex or money

I accidentally eat my dog's tiny hairs every day but I never feel sad

Some women feel sad about their pubic hair

How can you feel sad about your pubic hair?

Just wax that shit

Or get over it

Women should love themselves

Women should love their bodies

Women should be thin

Women should be curvy

Women should be pink

Women should be golden

Women should love themselves

When I was a child I used to pretend the salt & pepper shakers

were ballroom dancers & salt was always the girl

I'm scared when I have a kid I'll get really excited

& accidentally dress it like a hipster

The coconut smell of sunscreen

The coconut smell of burned skin

The place where they're building a highrise where all the white people

will live but the white people look askance & say

Where will the El Salvadorans go?

Other white people just really don't give a shit

because their property values will go up

Other white people look at their watches as the bus goes by

with tons of faces peering out

The day laborers on bicycles, smiling

Coconuts at the Latin Market

I'm scared to go to the botanica and speak Spanish

even though I can sort of speak Spanish

My accent isn't good enough

I'm scared to walk by myself at night anywhere

My mace isn't good enough

There should be alcohol at baby showers

Oh wait, there is alcohol at baby showers

Dogs should be able to get drunk

Dogs should be able to get high

My dog accidentally got high once & I was high too & I felt so guilty

I ate brownies & then I felt bad about it

I wasn't a hot wife

I wasn't any kind of wife

I was a blue storm on an orange afternoon

Take a picture of me

Take care, Said the lady at the grocery store to me after I wrote her a list

of affordable neighborhoods to live in in my hometown

It's the only city with close-together buildings

that doesn't make me want to kill myself

I love it

I should love it more than I love it

I should love it as much as everyone who still lives there loves it

But I shouldn't live there

The feeling of bricks on fingertips

The sounds of sleds on driveways

Sun on azaleas

Everyone's nice moms & weird moms & difficult moms & scary moms

What will I wear if I'm a mom?

I hope nothing too busty but also nothing too busy & nothing too blah

No puces, no peach

When I was a kid I would make things up

& then pretend back to myself

that I didn't make them up

Like I would dream something but then recast it in my head

as a memory or I'd read something & then think it actually happened

If I told myself the story enough times it was true

Like when I tried to do a Wiccan ritual

& burned a hole through my white rug

Well, that's actually true

Witches should not be thirteen

Witches should be like cobwebby lace with herbs, but in person form

Witches should be whatever they want to be

Witches should be free in the ocean

Like Michelle Williams at Heath Ledger's funeral

All wet & smiling in this way that killed me when I saw the pictures

Like grief could be something honeyed

that comes up from the bottom of your lungs

As much as it can be a plate of Saltines & a lump

under a sheet in a dark room

As much as it can be a memory totally erased

Like a series of months with a hole cut right straight through it

Like where's my head? Where did my head go?

It got pushed under

It got pushed over

It got a crown put on top of it

Not a tiara

Not a television

But a bright band forged

Right in the middle of it all

MOTEL BOULEVARD

We perform our faux sadness

when a fat actor dies of an overdose

We perform our full

allyship when the wrong verdict is delivered

We perform our sense

of injustice where everyone can see it

& we're colorblind

& we're outraged

& we're humbled

& we're thinking critically

& we're doing it out loud

&

All the recycling bins, overflowing with craft beer

bottles & fragility. The miniscule

rocks caught under the refuse

of the week.

FAT DAISIES

I was going to say that this is how America is:
a chain of fat daisies. Daisies because we're
ordinary, but we're also optimistic, you know?

But then I started thinking of blueberry blossoms
& the painted desert & the prairie thistle,
all these different roots digging down
into the network of gray ethernet cables
& fracking & foibles & fairies,
all the things that should be etched,
but aren't.

        Our coins should bear the brunt
of our daily lives, show a minivan
or a horseshoe or a nightstand
or something construction-related that probably
a toddler boy would know the name of, but I don't.
Something tall, that towers, that scares me when
it's above me, that makes me fearful for the men
who are on it in little metal boxes.

Those men are making
things in the likeness, in the always-afterness
of George Washington's triangular nose but making it bigger
& made of steel. We're all sitting here underneath,
hoping we can figure out how to jangle.

WILD EGG

Another gray day in the gray world;
I should be happy.

My stomach growling
with the dawn,
the two warm

bodies of my boyfriend & my dog;
the lumps I love.

Checking cervical mucus while
the neighbor children yell & carve
pumpkins & I feel more

& more flexible each afternoon.
Spinnbarkeit but *not yet not yet*
not enough money

cracking in my bones like bones
that crack in a beak. I believe

I am the marble
precipice or the place

where the grass is lying flat.
I smell some like honey
& some like fear.

ALL MY TURQUOISE

My closet full of scuffed cowgirl boots
& how I'll tell anyone who'll listen

about my soul's bright home in the desert,
how I kept turning my face again & again & again

to the sun, claiming my place whether I have
one or whether I do not.

Look at these leggings as pants &
bangs cut by girls with zines

or altars to Guadalupe in their kitchens. I'd
never make a zine because they seem

too earnest in a 90s punk rock way that I can't
own at all because I was in elementary school

when Kurt Cobain put a bullet in his beautiful
mouth. But I'll take all the Guadalupe that a white girl

born in Baltimore can take. Give me a robe
of roses. Crown me with stars. I used to jam

to mariachi music on a tape I thrifted
in Truth or Consequences because isn't that

how you make a life outside the norm? With
horns & moustaches & glittery pants while you

waggle your butt dancing around the kitchen,
cooking the food that is not of your ancestors?

I'll appropriate your culture & call it cool. That's
not a metaphor. It's the lesson of ages,

what I sucked into my body like vegan chia seed
pudding. *It's an honor,* you know, *not a mockery* because

look at all my Jewish hair that's not actually Jewish at all,
see my hamsa bracelet & all of the unironic opinions I gave about

circumcision in my Yiddish literature class.
That's the way to win friends & enemies.

When I speak of friends, I mean admirers. When
I speak of enemies, I mean cyber stalkers.

I'm the pinnacle of pinnacleism & I *make* the place.
I burrow out. I spread in. Move over.

TANG

The chalk-white sky
looks like a dryer sheet &
makes me feel like I am a dryer sheet.

Nothing under it can be clearly
seen or clearly felt— not the droopy
orange light of dawn settling on my
dog's ears, not my beige rental walls,
not my unshaven winter legs, not my
glitter nails or my shiny car or all the poems
sleeping inside my computer.

Most days I'm appalled
at the meanness in my own head.
But if I call myself out for being mean
in this poem, that shows
I'm not actually mean. Right?
Self-awareness is the new being-a-good-person.
Judgment is the new choosing sides.

I lie in bed yelling LOUDNESS & littering
the quilt with candy wrappers that look like
dirty snowflakes or goat fur or bath bubbles
or the weird warped control knobs on
a child's robot toy. My perception inks
& swells & grows & swims. I'm a mean girl wrapped
in a "mean girl" wrapped in a blanket.
I'm a pig in a blanket.

MILLENNIALIST

My naivete, my
inability to grieve
for every cause that's unjust is because
I had to un-color myself in to be an adult,
I had to let parts of my *red red red*-ness
                              shrivel & die
                              so I could be here
                              writing this poem
because a baby is a dollar sign
under the mantle of the milquetoast man you married,
because knowing better
isn't doing better
isn't feeling better,
because it doesn't come gold-plated
or silver-plattered.

Spoiled, snobby,
& thinking sadly
about my student's
thesis statement on President Obama,
because inherent classism
because basic bitch,
because I'm standing here with red blood
dripping out of my pretty nose
& expecting everyone to call me
a rose.

DON'T READ THE COMMENTS

Sloshing wave of OMG white girl love getting
Smashed together into the sand until the thin clavicles
Bang up against each other gesticulating madly
Tweeting torrent of clique fems bubble wrap women
Where everyone believes they're a bright star with
Something to say to really really say about their wonky
Vagina about their eyebrow hair about their fake eyelashes
About the sad baths they took in their sad bathtub about
Introvert power about thin privilege about fuck you thigh gap
About Peggy Olsen & her wide noble forehead like the map
They want to trace their lives on & send to Mars
So they can live forever

FROM ABOVE

All the people shitting in toilets at this very moment
& the water it takes to wash it away,
the pencils scratching & the cheap
clothes hanging
limp & bright under
lights everywhere

My fear of the growing & gathering,
like girl babies in China
mean anything to me
other than an injustice
I can read about, nodding
with my wrinkled
& concerned brow.

I'm scared of everything.
I'm scared of everywhere.

I admit it to myself
but never to the handshakers
with their firm, firm grip.

Shut up is what I want to say,
like hugeness
or multitude
is something to be scared of.
But isn't it?
Is it?

My biggest fear is that I'll die
before I have a child,
a fear amplified by articles
about the great gleaming
fissures in everything we've made,
the ice slipping from the crown
of the world.

Our earth will be
a charred husk of hell
in fifty years.

But I don't care because
I still want my baby.

I just want my baby,
& I'm selfish
& I know it
& I'll never be a righteous green woman
who pees out hormonal residue every month
so as not to clutter the planet.

I'll never be any kind of righteous woman
except maybe self-righteous, which I think
I'm supposed to apologize for—but to who?
I'm tired of saying sorry for my space.
I'm tired of taking back, of twinkling,

of lying awake thinking of ways to
enjoy exercise & achieve career goals,
slurping green juice, glugging yogurt.

This is not supposed to be a manifesto.
This is not supposed to be a critique.

This poem isn't *blink blink* flashing
signifying the boorish invasion
of civilization on our tender,
mewling little moment.

It's not the realization
of how bad &
blackly
we fucked up.

It's not
the siren
when it's starting.

POEM OF OUR MOMENT

Little boys I babysat for shouldn't be grown up on Facebook wearing
tuxedos & taking girls to proms or I guess they should,

I just shouldn't care or think it's weird in the way
that accidentally finding yourself really close to a stranger's butt

is weird. Is it bulbous? It is sufficiently clothed? I'm always
scared until it bends back up or scoots away although

I know our bodies are just bodies, are so much more
than bodies, are all we have, are nothing,

are the texts of our brains, are the theorized spaces
where fingerprints both begin & end. Ride or die, body of mine,

fucking ride or die. Be bloody or don't be bloody,
be in a mediated space or be the mediated object

that takes up space. Sneeze or puke or fuck or stay the hell still,
stay still. Run or bike or ballet yourself around the air you're in.

Or burn. Burn the body in the way it does or doesn't make sense
like "New Uses For Old Things" in *Real Simple* or the way

I want to be thinner, but not enough to actually do
anything about it & that's what makes me a perfect

American. Sitting at my computer lamenting
the innocence of a child who was a child ten years ago

is what solidifies my place as a woman of my age.
People I went to high school with shouldn't be doctors & lawyers yet,

because all of a sudden everyone on TV is younger than me
& I thought I still signed my life away to pepper-gray-haired guys,

not the lipglossed girls of the early 2000s, emoticons
I sneer at, sniff at, sweetening my own existence,

dissolving myself into manufactured drama just like an 8th
grade pool party, but without the hot dogs. At my own

8th grade pool party, I had reddened hair, slightly fat hips,
board shorts & a black bikini top. I remember everything

I ever wore or maybe I just think I do because there's pictures:
a tight jade green shirt I got drunk in every weekend,

denim skirts on denim skirts on denim skirts & then cowboy boots
& cowboy boys, vintage ponchos & limes. Then dirt. Good brown

dirt & mountains, a perpetual base tan with hair blowing in the air
just like a picture in my mind from a book. A book about a map

of the desert & then my soft-focus Old West fetish put up to prick
all the pinstriped people. Although they don't care; I'm the one

who thinks this narrative means something someone else
doesn't have because I used to have the thing I wanted, then I lost

it, then all I thought about was getting it back again except bigger,
except better, & this time with sparkles & penny tile & bright light

flowing backwards. If we took all the light from all the photographs
on all the Facebooks & pinned it to our chests,

it would be like the boutonniere of the internet. It would be like the
biggest best bouquet to blind us all.

DUMB BITCH

When women make me mad I call them "dumb bitch" in my head &
then I feel like a bad feminist because I shouldn't say bitch & I shouldn't
call other women dumb & then I feel mad at myself for making myself
feel bad & then I feel even more mad at myself because what I just said
sounds suspiciously like letting myself off the hook & then I feel

like I need to read up on choice feminism again & intersectionality &
Gloria Anzaldúa & "The Master's Tools Will Never Dismantle The
Master's House" & blog posts on white privilege oh & Judith Butler
because my understanding of performativity is not very nuanced &
yes I wore a miniskirt to the Apple Genius Bar on purpose & didn't
apologize to anyone for using a slice of thigh for better service, how to
reconcile my feminism with my vanity & how to reconcile my anger at
the feeling that I must reconcile rationally, like it mattered to anyone
that Oprah put poets in pretty dresses in her magazine like it means
something to print another article about the mom that masturbated
up against the washing machine versus the mom who masturbated
under her poplin skirt at her big mahogany desk like anyone thinks it's
important how I'm an activist or not an activist, like writing

shit on the internet about body image & fat-shaming means I'm putting
a prick in the patriarchy, like holding a woman's leg while she pushes
a baby out of her vagina in a hospital room above a street filled with
gray monuments & men in suits is part of how we innovate, like doing
something is doing anything is discourse, is debate, go ahead & pat
yourself on the back, ladies, eat your radical like candy, girls, swill it
like wine, have it fill & fill & fill & fill & fill.

JAM

Here are the things I like:
My boyfriend.
My dog.
Cooking stuff to eat & then eating it.
Singing really loudly to old Tanya Tucker songs
while I have headphones on:
Skin, fur, & salt
all in the delta dawn.

Everything else can go fuck itself
said the generalized anxiety disorder,
& the lonely wooden table
& all of the internet, every font
& every pixel. If I think I am
the internet, or if I live
inside the internet, that's the truth,
said the magical thinking;
not the kind with starshowers or sparkles,
but the kind of counting cracks & license plates
& the sudden, overwhelming majesty
of the strawberry's bulbous underside.
Nothing else.

THINSPO

I take my able-bodied

body to a place where we

can be alone. I almond meal

I crystal light I sports bra

eyeliner out lipstick up

image out image in

My Feminazi mouth

My baby oil breath

My size eyes

TWENTY ASSES

Sometimes I wish I wasn't so
materialistic & then I think, well,
that would be depressing.
Because nice things are nice
& I like them, crunching them up
in my hands & rubbing them
on my cheeks & even biting them
a little, sometimes. Just at the edges.
It's not like I'm an evil cartoon duck
rolling in money or anything.
Or Kim Kardashian.
Kim Kardashian would probably have
twenty asses if she could, just for the joy
of owning twenty asses. I totally
understand that joy but I want you to know
that I don't need the joy
on that scale. I just need good-quality
sheets & in-style jeans & cute teapots
that will fill me when I look at them.
Just let me have my little red teapot
of joy. I promise I won't let anyone
toss it into a landfill when I've used
up all its shininess. I swear it.

PHOBE MANIFESTO

Here's what I think about running a marathon:

Moving your body in one direction
for a really long time is just moving your body
in one direction for a really long time.

But I'll ooh & ahh over anyone's homegrown vegetables
or homesewn clothes or log cabin they built
with their admirably calloused hands.
I just don't care about your sustained athleticism.

It's not enough to have all the things or do all the things.
We have to show them to other people & look at their things, too.

Saying you're humbled is basically the opposite of being humbled &
I'll confess I'm ashamed by a lot of the mean things

in my brain. Like that certain people are just weird-looking,
no matter what, or that my boyfriend walks like a crab

or that I think you really should have tried harder
to breastfeed. But I'm scared to say mean things
in public even though all I do is say stuff from my computer

& get money for it,
pretending to stamp out the patriarchy by critiquing
Katy Perry & her boobs that have gone beyond
being costumed as cupcakes & are now
actual cupcakes.

The discourse of what to eat & how to eat & where to work
& how to work when I feel sloppy & spoiled

because I don't want to wear pumps or get tenure
or eat macaroni from a box. But I want everyone else
to be able to do those things if they want to do them

so I write like a heart with spikes & I think my meanness deep
inside like a kitchen faucet that'll cut your lip right off.

We're iridescent, I tell myself, *We're multifaceted.* I know you
are telling yourself this, too, at the beginning of every

frowning magenta afternoon opening a sad desk salad
or trying to get the digital word out about abortion.

Then we're making dreamcatchers with strands of our own hair
or tooling a maze of a leather belt or chanting the names

of our future children like talismans on our tongues or imagining up
some dreamy opus where we're constantly getting fucked

& smiling about it because there's no male privilege
or vaginismus. Then we're not. This is how the world ends:

not with a bomb or a sun that's scorched
those melty icecaps but with an ovary
& an asterisk.
Or a sneaker
dipped in gold.

SOMEONE ELSE'S BODY

This is the only thing
that's true:

   everyone
here, all of us on this big-ass
blue ball, started life
deep in the dark
of someone else's
precious,
precious
body

& then we came out
in some way, because
we had to, because it
was time. Now
we are doing what we do,
whatever it is: wearing denim,
texting excuses, teaching students
how to make grammatically-correct sentences,
tilling a field or typing a spreadsheet or
feeling the slim cock of a gun
against our meaty thighs
or choking black men until their breath is gone

   & we are not
the same. All of us are terrible
animals & some of us
are even worse.

I have a million jobs & so
does that girl & that guy & that middle-aged
man who won't stop twitching his lips.
I don't believe in God but at night
behind my eyes I keep seeing a ghostly,
gigantic hand picking me up & putting me
down, like I'm a doll in a dollscape,

a beautiful white doll like the beautiful
white dolls that lined my bedroom
when I was a child, glass eyes
& gluey smell.
I sit here worried about the size
of my pores, the HTML tags
I can't get right, the life that's not unfolding
the way the spinning ballerina said it would,
or the way that meets
   the movie in my mind.

Elsewhere, a man is doing his job.
Another man is doing another job in another place.
It's afternoon; a boy lies facedown
in the street,
   in the sun.

A woman has a red baby & a gray baby
emerge from a stapled slit above her pubic
bone. Another woman makes a list,
inscribes a tally.
It's getting longer.
The din is rising.

I try to speak my outrage but my tongue's
thick & dumb, a rubber bullet
ricocheting in a bubble.
A big old pearly bubble.
Our privilege: opalescent.

  Nothing is the same.

WHY WHITE PEOPLE LOVE "REMIX TO IGNITION"

I don't drink coffee anymore because it makes
me scared & not in a good way,
not the way it used to be, when we just danced & danced
& danced with our hair in salty sweat streaks,
before the twin beasts of anything we could ever have dreamed
of took over, the plump arms of our future babies
or our desperate need to be each other & not to be
each other, to live the way we wanted but also
get shiny & be shiny & make something
we could feel, touch, taste, breathe on & breathe in.

There's so many things you need for a good life,
they told me, or I bought this from them, or I wanted to buy
this from them, or you did & I followed your lead
like we were all having the same conniptions or
smiling in a knowing way or fighting because we were
different but in some parts we were the same
in loving a rape apologist or ten of them
but it was prom & it was the song
the song the song the song, it was the sun or
my hair that wouldn't lie flat, won't ever lie flat
or my fear of getting fat or the tiny buzzing
in my head that doesn't ever stop saying where does art
end & fun begin, when can we enjoy what we see
because we know x is bad & y is bad & z is the literature
about it so don't act like you don't understand the hegemonic,
the hedging, or the way things are sharp & sharpening,
the volume how it's going up & up & up.

UNICORN

I've been so busy licking spoons of ice cream & looking at moccasins on the internet & tweezing my nipple hairs that I forgot to cry about how much I hate modern society.

Because it is mean, right? It is the huge bearded lumberjack of capitalism stomping on happiness in a mad, plaid way. Or it's the shining sequined dress that strangles or suffocates, one glitzy disc at a time. My eyes are telescopes. My breasts are teacups. My teeth can be chewed into gum & then smacked back again into teeth, guarding the pincushion of my tongue.

I wear jackets & I wear tights. I wear boots & I wear panties.

I wear everything I own at once & then I strip it off so you can watch.

MOON CHART

I refuse

to hate

my body.

This is a political stance.

Oppression is forever

is what it feels like,

trying to convince

anyone

that agency for women

is more than a birth control

pill dissolving on the white

funk of worker's tongues,

or that dismantling

isms is more grit

than a WELCOME sign.

Still, I want to be

the perfect

kind of white girl

to truly velvet out

the plush jewelbox

of my Middle American girlhood

the right kind of white girl

who says the right things

solidarity & justice & hashtag activism

without claiming the pain

of the colonial & painting it

as badge, banner,

conflation & key.

Conflation as key.

Silver lock.

Lock you have to lick

open, lock that eats,

lock that ribbons the

glassy perfection of

credit cards or the

antique beauty of

skeletons. Lock

that's locked.

Keys we keep.

This amazing

anorexia.

NINE STRAND

The shiny beetle dead under
the door is made of a green as
green as green can be. I want to be

rolled in dirt & planted,
push back up with the begonias
& lost toy soldiers. When untied,

we're all as free as you
thought we could be. Look, raffia ribbons.
Thank god for the soft bindings,
you know? Thank god

for our plump mouths holding words
like sour, spitty lozenges.
Our blue lips. Our knotted braids.

ALEXANDRIA TO WARRENTON

When I yawn, I think I look like a
jack-o-lantern. When the evening light is
shining behind him, through his
ears, and his ears are pink.
When we roll our souls
down the street. When we flap our
tongues. When we turn on the water
so no one can hear us pee. When the swirls
of the wood tell me a secret. When I drink coffee
& then can't eat, when the humidity feels
like everyone I've ever hated spitting
on my skin. When the sun is there & when
the moon is not there. When every neighbor
has seen me bobbleheaded, braless,
when every neighbor has been me
yelling in the night & sweating
in the morning. When the smear
of fingerprint on the windowpane
is a map. It's always a map.

MT. VERNON AVENUE

I want to protect my dog
when he goes to pee on a pricker bush
like I want to punch the guy whose eyes
follow my ass in pajama pants.
It's cold. It's grey.
It's morning. I want to
be left alone but also coddled &
cuddled up in a comforter covered
in dog hair & fed hot chocolate
through a twirly straw by someone
who understands that all of this
is bullshit. Right? I mean, come
on. Right?

I'm mad & confused but I think mainly
I'm a bursting ball of bright red
spun to think she's the center of
the ice, but there's no ice.
There's still no goddamn ice out here.

BLUELAND

Women like the Dallas airport
bejeweled but also kinda country
I'm awake now because of these things
& I'm full up because of these things
my eyes glazing all jetlag pride
my greasy eyelids   The monumental white feet
of men in gym socks & men
with khakis just a hair too short
their vulnerable ankles   their needy knees
the terrible mightiness of the online payment system
the arrogant moony teeth of everyone who isn't me
all trench-coated   all spray-on hair
the top part of the old person's gums
when they smile & a baby's soft spot
how it feels fluttery & freaky   excess droplets
of pee leftover on the toilet seat like a library book
with a roach pressed in it or a hospital scene
without the movie lights   my naughty bits
my swoony parts   eating food   wearing dresses
kissing kids   sitting up straight & depilating   whoa
all the exotic messengers
all our sticky hands

LEDGE & HAMMER

The itchy truth:

I wanted to objectify the slim-hipped muscly guy who
was so handsome in a trashy way but I wanted to be politically

correct. What am I doing to my body by holding in my pee all the
time, sunbathing although I know exactly what a skin cancer mole

looks like? What do I do with all of this dark gray fear? I always
thought it would be red & fiery but instead it creeps up & plays

forever like the *Unsolved Mysteries* theme song that terrorized
my childhood. I'm the definition of white people problems &

the whole ironic bits that blow up with it, settling as eyes roll back
in their heads. I'm falling asleep as I tell me to myself again & again

The night light is on as his & hers scroll by. When it's all over, if it
ever is, the list is going to be long. When they dig us up,

we'll all want to be the best kind of fossil,
the most valuable bone.

ROYGBIV

The world keeps folding

in on itself & then outwards

smelling like pumpkin flavored syrup

& then moss. I keep trying to look at

the big big picture. I say to Mark

this book needs some nice poems,

some positive poems about humanity

& he says *yes, that's what I've been trying to tell you*

but I can't just say but all of us are really good at heart

or some other pale truism when I watch a video of a woman's

vagina being cut twelve times while she's giving birth,

while she says *NO* as clearly as *NO* can be heard,

when I am told over & over & over again to hate my female body

& believe that my female body is bad, flawed, fat, silly, lemoned:

when I don't believe these things, these stories

about what is absolute & what is fluid.

These crackles in consciousness.

There are no bows for this.

There is no moral here:

in our fonty sea of fake sympathy & manufactured outrage,

so many people trying so hard to be their own goddamn rainbow.

One thing tastes like dollar store cream soda & then it all does

& all of us get vaccinated & none of us own guns & everyone

on the planet goes to the same school & the internet is free

& everyone's genitals remain intact & GMOs are burned to a crisp

under the spacelights of NASA & the water flows & the sun shines

& the soldiers come home & all of our smiles are gold,

but a new kind of gold that's more gold

than gold has ever been before.

We are grateful,

then, we are so blisteringly grateful

& still we worship at the altar of our own perceived pain

& at the altar of the perceived pain of our neighbors:

the tiny baby under the jaundice lights in the NICU,

the sudden heart attack on the highway, kickstarting

with our wallets a vast & beautiful chain

of human love to human love.

Wait, I think this poem turned into the poem Mark wanted but

it's still not the poem that I want. Let's bet our gold

teeth that the reviews of this book will say it's too meta

in its movements, too broad in its assumptions.

It's a white girl's book about being a white girl.

All true. All so true. I try to unwrite

we and our but I don't know how except to

say I am just as guilty, just as bullshit, treading water

as hard here in the heart of my heart,

writing these meta-ass winding poems

that really won't do anything for anyone

in their pronouncements, with their

sloping little endings that are intended

to ring in your ears & your ears &

your ears. There's my dog's tiny

flaccid penis against my hand as I carry

him outside to shit, here in a city where

I can actually see the stars.

There's my laptop on my lap,

killing all the eggs in my ovaries,

which I imagine as pearls shriveling

into ash. There's my twoheart &

my threeheart & my eighty-eightheart.

Here it is: my heart.

SUNKIST

I believe in a time
where sun is what the fat
girls do & the sweat

of bellies on the long grass
is all the slick we'll need
to get through next week like the
metaphysical light that surrounds

your head, even when I'm crying
& even when I'm yelling,
bellowing, cow-

flared nostrils. My song
is loud & planetary.

Tomorrow's made of meat.

LITTLE HAIRS

I see the pink of a late-summer rose
& think *that would be a pretty lipstick shade*
instead of *oh the majesty of the natural world*
so there goes my hippie card even though
I can still revel in the buttwarm eggs just out
of the hens in the streaky dawn.

All I want is a tablespoon of dew &
myself with perfectly mussed hair
looking plucky in oversized boots,
holding the scene within my mind;
the little corny campfire of my narcissism.
In the periphery, other happy people:
but blurred.

If I put my narcissism
into the shiny box with everyone else's
narcissism what will be there to make
her happy, if the other narcissisms
are worrying about themselves,
hurriedly smoothing back their own
little hairs? We can't shower our
selves with the scented pages of catalogs.
We can't muddy anything. We can't
look past to the petals
while we tenderly cup our own
small flame.

IDEA OF A ROAD

It's a night when all the books in all the damn
libraries are opening softly like wings, rustling
along while the world's most luxurious car is telling
its driver how to get home. In 500 feet, make a right
turn. In 1000 feet, bear left. Your home is about
to offer itself to you. Will you take it?

I don't think I will. Why can't the road be a long,
long tongue that takes me out & away, the guidebooks
stacked on the backseat splattering wildly on the floor
of the car at every gorgeous neon fast-food sign we just
have to photograph with our phones? The road is not a road
but it's an idea of a road. A book is not a book but a screen
for a book, a screen that shines its light when the moon
is hidden, every flat black night.

At McDonald's we ordered iced tea that was made with
salt instead of sugar & we spat dramatically out
the sides of our mouths, onto the concrete by the car.
We still talk about it. I've never learned
to make good iced tea, not like my grandmother
or the little old women in half-aprons in cabin restaurants
in places like Alabama, but I don't need to, do I?
Iced tea is there whether I make it or not.
A house is there whether you build it or buy it.

Can we keep going? Past all this? Out to a field where we'll
turn a barn into a library & live off the land, me with my basket
full of berries & you with an axe to cut the light in two.

SCARF

The trees
are locked together, stormy-
eyed &

with a windy red melody,
my eardrums bleeding.

I have climbed & been climbed
beside the bedside table & the
dirtiest sheets with my sweat-

stained shirt on the floor.
My limbs are less
& I thumbprint.
I copy myself over,

the dead middle of
the bandana's fold.

RECEIPTS

I killed a stinkbug by drowning it
in lavender lotion from Anthropologie. All

around, the vintage suitcases I collected
during the dark times. Up with the crinoline

& the linen curtains that make us feel safe
with good taste. Sailor pants in the

drawer for a nautical Halloween costume.
Hair in braids. Girls putting bikini

pictures on the internet from their phones.
Girls speaking in videos about their

plastic drawers filled with shimmers for
the eyes. Those wavy lines televisions

never get anymore. My shorts are too
short but also not short enough,

not for this place, this night, this
crawling sense I wear with

claws. Shirts about alma maters &
squinty sodas with straws floating up

while I'm still blueing
my way in & then out.

AKELA FLATS

Cotton candy birth control,
red-white-&-blue sunglasses,
firework dental floss.

This is America.

I thought we all wanted
different things,
but
we don't.

We're all mock-twisted-beautiful
with our bellies busted open,
looking at each other
under the sun

as bright as we can
as bright as we damn well can.

ACKNOWLEDGEMENTS

The journals, magazines and websites where these poems first appeared: *NOÖ*, *Hobart*, *Everyday Genius*, *Punchnel's*, *Big Lucks*, *The Bakery*, *ILK*, *Stoked*, *Jellyfish*, *Gabby*, *H_NGM_N*, *Entropy*, *By The Slice*, *Word Riot*, and *Whiskeypaper*.

Starry Night Residency in Truth or Consequences, New Mexico, where I spent ten days shivering in atypical Southern NM cold, eating pastries, and writing some of these poems.

All of my friends and family but most of all Randall, who doesn't "get" poetry but whose ongoing patience and love bolsters me every day.

Melanie Sweeney Bowen, Gina Abelkop, Jordan Scott, Robert Alan Wendeborn (my poetry BFF), and Connie Voisine, who took time out of their busy lives to read this book.

Sandra Simonds, Kristen Stone, and Carmen Giménez Smith, whose comments on the book were invaluable.

Most of all, an infinity of thank yous and heart eyes to Mark Cugini, whose trust, vigilance, patience, and constant effervescent enthusiasm made this book possible.

ABOUT THE AUTHOR

Carrie Murphy is the author of the poetry collection *Pretty Tilt*. She received an MFA from New Mexico State University. Originally from Baltimore, MD, Carrie works as a teacher, freelance writer, and doula in Albuquerque, NM. *Fat Daisies* is her second book.

ALSO FROM BIG LUCKS BOOKS

Wastoid, by Mathias Svalina

Wildlives, by Sarah Jean Alexander

Pink Museum, by Caroline Crew

Dear S., by Rachel E. Hyman

Isn't That You Waving At You, by Elizabeth Clark Wessel

And I Shall Again Be Virtuous., by Natalie Eilbert